Endorsements:

I have known Joe and Stephanie for more than twenty years, and have ministered in marriage conferences several times with them. Their testimony of marriage restoration against all odds is extremely powerful and refreshing. In the current divorce culture, it is very encouraging to read a story of God's redemption for a marriage that no one thought could be healed.

If you are struggling in your marriage, this book will greatly encourage you and embolden your faith in the living God to supernaturally heal your marriage just as He did for Joe and Stephanie. However, I encourage you not to only think of yourself, but to always have on hand several copies of the DeMott's book, *Redemption*, to give to other couples in need.

Craig Hill
Founder - Family Foundations International
www.familyfoundations.com

Joe and Stephanie have condensed in this booklet the miraculous healing of their lives, marriage and family. This miraculous bending, blending and restoring of their lives, marriage and family has given hope to many as a result of their travels worldwide. Their transparency of the process of their own healing, through God's grace by faith in His word has given birth to hope in the hearts and lives of many over the years who have seen similar miracles in their lives, marriages homes and families. Their prayer and ours is that the Lord may be pleased to use their testimony to spark the same hope, faith and healing in the hearts of many that, "with God nothing shall be impossible"!

Lou Montecalvo
Founding and Overseeing Pastor of Redeemer Ministries
www.redeemertemple.com

We met Joe and Stephanie DeMott several years ago in conjunction with ministry efforts of one of the ministries with which we cooperate. Although each restored couple's restoration story is unique we found that our journeys to restoration and healing were similar in many ways. We have spent a lot of time on several occasions "comparing notes" and praising God for what He has done in all of our lives and especially for our marriage restorations.

Joe and Stephanie have a compelling testimony of what God can accomplish in a devastated marriage if either the husband or wife will choose to believe in and hold fast to their covenant marriage vows. Their commitment to marriage healing and restoration for not only themselves but all marriages that they can touch is a calling from God. They are truly missionaries to marriages around the world.

Don't read their story just as one of how badly two people can treat each other in the midst of marital strife. Instead read it for the glory they give God for His protection, guidance and safe keeping on their journey back from the brink.

Rex and Carolyn Johnson
Directors
Covenant Keepers Inc.
www.covenantkeepersinc.org

"I've heard many testimonies of marital redemptions over the years. Joe and Stephanie's is one of most dramatic. Moving from abuse and adultery to love and strong covenant is truly a miracle of God. I pray that reading this booklet will be a turning point for many couples facing similar situations. God does indeed raise the dead!"

R. Loren Sandford,
Senior pastor New Song Church and Ministries (Denver, Colorado), author, prophetic voice and conference speaker.
www.newsongchurchandministries.org

Ezekiel 37 New King James Version (NKJV)

The Dry Bones Live

The hand of the LORD came upon me and brought me out in the Spirit of the LORD, and set me down in the midst of the valley; and it *was* full of bones. ² Then He caused me to pass by them all around, and behold, *there were* very many in the open valley; and indeed *they were* very dry. ³ And He said to me, "Son of man, can these bones live?" So I answered, "O Lord GOD, You know."

⁴ Again He said to me, "Prophesy to these bones, and say to them, 'O dry bones, hear the word of the LORD! ⁵ Thus says the Lord GOD to these bones: "Surely I will cause breath to enter into you, and you shall live. ⁶ I will put sinews on you and bring flesh upon you, cover you with skin and put breath in you; and you shall live. Then you shall know that I *am* the LORD."

⁷ So I prophesied as I was commanded; and as I prophesied, there was a noise, and suddenly a rattling; and the bones came together, bone to bone. ⁸ Indeed, as I looked, the sinews and the flesh came upon them, and the skin covered them over; but *there was* no breath in them. ⁹ Also He said to me, "Prophesy to the breath, prophesy, son of man, and say to the breath, 'Thus says the Lord GOD: "Come from the four winds, O breath, and breathe on these slain, that they may live." ¹⁰ So I prophesied as He commanded me, and breath came into them, and they lived, and stood upon their feet, an exceedingly great army

We speak that your marriage will be healed and whole also!

Redemption

By

Joe and Stephanie DeMott

A Story of Faith, Covenant Grace and Mercy

2 Corinthians 2:14 (NKJV)
Now thanks be to God who always leads us in triumph in Christ, and through us diffuses the fragrance of His knowledge in every place.

Redemption

We wanted to write this booklet in a form that we could express our individual feelings of our journey with you. Many couples in this situation need answers. We encourage you to go to God for your answers. Know no one knows your spouse better than He does. No one wants you to be healed more than He does. We hope our testimony will bring hope and encouragement where ever you are in your marriage.

Genesis 2:23-25 (NKJV)
And Adam said: "This is now bone of my bones and flesh of my flesh; She shall be called Woman,
Because she was taken out of Man."

Joe: In Revelations 12:11 the Word says "And they overcame him by the blood of the lamb and the word of their testimony." We want you to know God's Word is true. He's done things for us we know, He'll do in your marriage. He wants us all to be healed and whole with joy in our marriage, not clinging together without any hope. God wants to put love in our hearts and refresh us day by day. We know from what He's healed us from He can do the same for you.

Revelation 12:11 (NKJV)
And they overcame him by the blood of the Lamb and by the word of their testimony, and they did not love their lives to the death.

<u>Stephanie</u>: God's Word clearly says He is not a respecter of people. As Joe stated what God has done in our lives we have seen Him do in many other people's lives. He desires wholeness for those who are hurting. Someone who is in a situation of hurting and despair you can give this testimony to them to encourage them also. Joe shared when we first met each other I was a believer and he was not. Our relationship started out unequally yoked. In God's word there are clear guidelines that tell us light and dark don't mix. We are to choose a mate that is also a believer in Jesus. Some don't even understand what it is to be equally yoked. It's to have the common denominator of knowing the Lord Jesus Christ as your personal savior. We didn't have that in our relationship.

2 Corinthians 6:14
Do not be unequally yoked together with unbelievers. For what fellowship has righteousness with lawlessness? And what communion has light with darkness?

Joe: Being unequally yoked was one of the first things we had to repent of. It was difficult to go back and repent from even getting married in the first place. We had also been involved sexually with each other before marriage. The sin we talk of set us up to fail from the start. It caused a lack of respect for one another. Maybe we were never supposed to have been married to each other. We know for sure we were wrong to get married at the time since I was not a Christian. Now we are in Covenant. We need to honor where we are.

I remember back when we first started going together, Stephanie was a Christian. I thought I was a Christian. I thought I knew who Jesus was, I knew who God was. I was brought up in a religious home but did not have a personal relationship with Jesus. I was getting on the police departments cadet program. I figured the fact I was doing well for society meant I was saved and I was going to go to heaven. I've gone to policeman's funerals where that is exactly what they tell you at the funeral. You're a cop and you're going to heaven. Look at this guy he did his duty. Now he's going to heaven. That's really the way I thought it would be my works would get me to heaven. But throughout the first years of our married life I had begun to abuse Stephanie. Actually the abuse happened even before we were married. I abused her physically, mentally and emotionally. As I got onto the police department I had a gun readily available to me all the time. I would actually threaten her. Threaten to kill her, threaten to kill myself, to get a reaction from her. I was craving something in my life. At the time I didn't know what it was. But now obviously as we look back we know it was the love of the Lord I really did crave. Through wanting something more and wanting to control my life I was doing all these harmful things to my wife. Believe it or not, not even realizing how bad I was hurting her.

Stephanie: Each one of us has a desire in our heart to be loved. Everyone wants to be wanted and received by someone. When you start out a relationship where there's so much rejection involved it's hard to have hope. We want to say now God can take rejected people and put love in their hearts. Give them the love of the Lord. Take all the rejection off of you and give you love. The Lord paid the price for us. He took the rejection for us so we don't have to bear and feel it in ourselves. Joe was sharing we were two totally different people. We were totally opposite in so many ways. Joe was a real outspoken person. I was very shy and inward. I had never really known how to handle what was going on in our marriage. The abuse and violence was happening in front of our three small children. I had prayed for eight years that God would save Joe, that Jesus would change our lives. I prayed there would be restoration. I prayed Joe would become a Christian, but when we first got married I didn't do it God's way. I did it my own way. The Word tells us there's only one way. It's to do it God's way. When we go off and do our own thing we're asking for problems.

Proverbs 14:12 (NKJV)
There is a way that seems right to a man, But its
end is the way of death.

    I had this idea okay I'm going to believe. I'm going to marry Joe and he's going to be saved because of my belief. When it didn't happen in my timing I began to really resent Joe, to resent our children, to even resent God. Many times we can't admit when we're angry at God. He knows our heart. He already knows we're angry with him. So if you're in that position you need to open your heart up. Repent so the enemy won't be able to come in and cause you to enter into a greater sin. Really that's what happened with me, when my heart became hard. Over the years of abuse the hardness kept building layer upon layer. Soon I resented God. I felt like God, you don't hear and you don't answer in my timing. The resentment got so strong I ended up turning my back on God and going off into the world. I went into drugs, alcohol and also into adultery. Totally losing everything I had with the Lord, losing my relationship with Him. I was in a real valley situation.

Joe: Stephanie talks about being involved in adultery. Well in my situation I had also been involved in adultery. I followed the world's ways. I followed the ways of the world maybe even possibly what I thought was part of my profession. It was the macho thing to do. There was peer pressure from some. It was something I felt I had to do to be accepted. That's what we all want. We all want to be accepted whether it's by our peers or loved ones. It was something I fell into. It's something we see so much of now, not only in the world, but in the body of Christ. The enemy uses sin to tear marriages apart in so many ways. We are telling you today no matter whether it is adultery or abuse the blood of Jesus can cover those sins, cover the hurt and will heal you.

Stephanie talked about going through all this pain. I look back on it, like I said before I did not really know how damaging the things I was doing were to my marriage. I worked a lot; I brought home good money. I thought that's what was going to make my life happy, make my wife happy. I thought providing made me a good husband. I didn't realize the importance of nurturing my family spiritually and the harm I was causing. I thought money was all there was to providing.

Stephanie: The real problem was Joe didn't have a personal relationship with the Lord. There's a difference between what he talked about before, works and actually knowing Jesus as your savior. Because of Joe not having the Lord as his savior he didn't know how to be the head of our house. He didn't know how to protect and cover me the way the Word tells us in the book of *Ephesians Chapter 5:22-33*. A husband is to be a covering over his wife. Without first committing to Christ he couldn't really be the covering or protection to the family. With his profession, dealing with so many demonic things on the street, soon he started bringing those things home. The violence became a part of him. There wasn't a separation between going to work and coming home. It all blended with each other. It caused us to be in a downward spiral in our marriage.

Ephesians 5:25 (NKJV)
Husbands, love your wives, just as Christ also loved the church and gave Himself for her

Joe: As Stephanie shared as a spiral motion took place there was no stopping it. The abuse got worse, everything started getting worse. Stephanie said she started to look other places. To say she went off into adultery and went to look for somebody else seems pretty simple to say, but that's not really the way it happened. The way it happened was the more abuse I put into the relationship the more she would harden her heart against me to keep from being hurt. The more she hardened her heart to me, the more she was hardening her heart to the Lord. The Word of God really couldn't get access to her heart. She had people praying for her. There were women that were trying to encourage her, but a lot of them were encouraging her the wrong way. Even in the church the advice was to get rid of that guy, find somebody else. God has somebody better for you. Well God did have somebody better for her. God wanted me being saved, delivered and healed by His power.

That's who God had for her, but through the abuse she was going through and the advice she was getting, she gave up. I don't think there's anybody out there that can fault her. You would have to have known the torment I was putting her through to really understand the situation. Maybe you are or have gone through similar things in your life; if you have then you understand what God did for us. That's why we are here today, to tell you Jesus can heal those things for you.

<u>Stephanie</u>: In James 4:7, "Submit unto God. Resist the devil and he must flee." Many of us may understand the first part of the scripture. Or maybe you totally disregarded it. You're trying to get the devil to flee away, but you're not submitting to God. Really in our marriage relationship in so many ways I wasn't totally submitted to God. I was expecting God to answer me even though I had been disobedient in marrying Joe and other ways in my walk with the Lord.

I wanted God to instantly fix this mess. In this society we expect everything to be instant. When we sow, we reap. We can't expect God to instantly always pull us out of our messes. We have to look at what we did to cause what happened. Repentance is so important. I think you can take the word submit and put the word repent. Repent unto God, resist the devil and he must flee because that's part of submitting. Submission many times requires repentance.

2 Chronicles 7:14 (NKJV)
If My people who are called by My name will humble themselves, and pray and seek My face, and turn from their wicked ways, then I will hear from heaven, and will forgive their sin and heal their land.

<u>Joe</u>: I saw Stephanie basically go downhill from there, I don't mean to sound flippant, but I saw my wife as a sweet person. There were things I saw in her I really loved. I guess I didn't really know I loved them until they started to slip away. I started to see her heart was getting hard towards me, towards God. Even though before I never really cared now all of a sudden I did care. It started to dawn on me I was losing my wife. I was losing my marriage and my kids. I started to look to the Lord at that point. The reality she didn't love me had started to come out. She actually said, "I don't love you anymore." I remember the time she said that to me. What a piercing blow that was to me, not only to my heart and my spirit, but to my ego as well. My wife didn't love me anymore was really a hard blow to receive. I started to look to the Lord at that point and I did get saved. I asked God into my heart, I asked Jesus Christ to be my personal savior. I don't think I really understood the full impact of what that meant on my life. I started to get into God's Word even though it was mostly on Christian radio, a little bit of Christian T.V. here and there. The word started to get into my

heart. We know the Word does not return void, and that's what started to happen to me.

Isaiah 55:11 (NKJV)
¹¹ So shall My word be that goes forth from My mouth;
It shall not return to Me void,
But it shall accomplish what I please,
And it shall prosper in the thing for which I sent it.

Philippians 1:6 (NKJV)
⁶ being confident of this very thing, that He who has begun a good work in you will complete it until the day of Jesus Christ;

<u>Stephanie</u>: At first I felt like Joe was using my whole background with the Lord. I felt he was holding the bible to my head. The same way he held a gun to my head. I felt like he was using it as a tool of control. The reality was he really started seeking God and hearing God's word. Even though over the years I had tried to get him interested in going to church with me and sometimes he would go. This time it was real.

Before this change I think he totally turned his heart off. He really didn't hear anything. Maybe his spirit was receiving these seeds, but his heart was hard and he was rejecting the word. He began turning on Christian T.V., listening to Christian radio and at one point even started attending my church. At this time I wasn't attending church anymore. As he started to renew his mind a change started happening within him. It first started out as a manipulative act I feel. Joe thought okay she was always religious, by the way, religion means back to bondage. He didn't really understand a personal commitment with Jesus, but he was searching. As he went to church and heard the Word, he had a void in his heart. He realized something was missing in his life. He really truly did get saved. It wasn't a controlling act anymore to keep me in line.

Joe: I remember a lot of times I would feel frustration. I could only feel the hurt and pain. Knowing she didn't love me anymore was difficult. The fact we were probably going to get a divorce was hard to deal with. All these things were going through my mind. I asked Jesus to help me. I asked Him to bring peace in my heart. Please don't let me feel the pain. When I would stop and remember to ask Him to do those things for me He answered my prayers.

I think when my relationship with Jesus really started to grow because I saw He really cared, He did listen to me. He was helping me through everything no matter what would happen. I started to believe my marriage could be healed even though all the circumstances didn't show that to be a reality.

The circumstances were horrible to think about. All the things we were going through as well as the past abuse.

Hebrews 11:1 (NKJV)
Now faith is the substance of things hoped for, the evidence of things not seen.

We had psychologists and psychiatrists tell us "hey forget it there is no way you can get over all you've done to each other". And not only worldly psychologists, but Christian psychologists told us the same thing. God's word was powerful. I started to believe God's word and believe He cared about my family and cared about our relationship. Stephanie did not believe He could heal our family or I would change. I started to do the spiritual warfare it took. Everybody told me "it's her free will and she doesn't have to come back if she doesn't want to." But why do we pray for people to be saved? They don't have to be saved if they don't want to, but we continually pray.

We pray for our loved ones. We pray for God's will. We pray for God to use circumstances to soften their hearts. So I started to pray. The word in Proverbs 21:1 says, "The King's heart is in the hand of the Lord, as the rivers of water he turneth it wherever he wants to." And that's what I started to do. I prayed for God to take Stephanie's heart to move it back towards Him.

Stephanie: God is ultimately in control no matter how much we may mess up our lives, if we allow Him – if we give Him the right to intervene He will. If we lay it all down that's the main thing, you have to lay it down and let God pick it up.

As long as you have your hand on it and you're still trying to fix it, it's not going to get fixed. Just lay it on the altar and say okay Lord, I can't make this marriage work, I can't fix it, but you can. He knows better. He knows your spouse better than you do. He knows you even better than you know yourself. As I saw this change in Joe at first I thought he was totally a nutcase and they should lock him away in an institution. I felt he was totally a fanatic. My heart at that point was hard towards God. And he'd come to me with the word and give me scriptures. I'd think this guy is totally off his rocker. He's missing a few screws. They should lock him up. Actually I was even more afraid because I thought now he's even more dangerous. You hear stories about religious fanatics going off the deep end. I thought he truly had jumped off the deep end. Once I saw him surrender to Jesus, not just quoting scriptures at me. I actually saw a change in his life. I saw the Lord begin to transform him.

It appeared to be real. At first it wasn't. I had a restraining order on him. I had filed for divorce. When I would have contact with him at first sometimes he would still lose it and get angry. I thought well he hasn't changed. He's a bigger nut now than before. A year went by then two years passed by I saw a true change, a lasting change. There was a true heart change, in him. I could do things to try to get a reaction out of him. He wouldn't have a reaction. The peace of God was in his heart. The circumstances weren't overwhelming him, but he was trusting in God.

<u>Joe</u>: The restraining order Stephanie talked about was kind of a funny one, if you can take that as being funny. Here we were with this restraining order, but we could speak to each other. I could go over to the house as long as Stephanie said it was okay. As long as Stephanie felt good about it, but as soon as she didn't then I had to leave.

I remember this one particular time when we were separated, Stephanie was living at the house. I showed up we got in an argument at the door. Stephanie told me to leave. I left, Stephanie called the police. Here I was a Denver policeman waiting for the Westminster Police to come and arrest me. It could have been quite embarrassing. There I was,

I remember leaving the house thinking oh Jesus you gotta help me I can't get fired. If I get fired I won't even have a job to take care of my family, when we do get back together. I remember getting into the car and looking in the rear view mirror. As I looked down the street I saw the two Westminster police cars. They drove right past my street. I thought this is great, God blinded their eyes. They can't even find the house. It gave me enough time to get away. I look back knowing God was protecting me. He knew He needed to be there to protect me. There were all kinds of different situations where we saw God's hand move on our life. God always was proving His Word was true. I remember another situation where Stephanie and the kids had moved. They were living with the alien as I called him. Stephanie said this was it. I'm going to marry this other person. I was in the house at this particular time, in our home, and she was there in the alien's apartment with the kids. I thought man I can't handle this God.

God you saved me and you've delivered me from so much. How can this keep happening? Why can't she see I'm different and why can't we be together? I was praying calling her name "Stephanie, Stephanie". Well the enemy started coming in with all these thoughts of suicide. The demonic oppression was so heavy I had to see something happen before I could go on. I thought, I'm going to kill myself. I can't take this anymore! I remember sitting on my bed, taking my gun and putting it in my mouth. Thinking this is it, I'm going to do it and it'll all be over. I won't feel this pain anymore. I remember that I thought I have to give her one last chance. I have to talk to her one last time. I went ahead and I picked up the telephone. I started to dial the number she was at. There was no dial tone. All of a sudden I could hear her voice on the other side saying hello, hello. I thought this is really strange. I said hello and asked how come you're on the phone it didn't have time to ring yet? She said, "how come you're not answering the phone?" I've been trying to call you there's no answer." Well I didn't know the bell was turned off on the telephone. All this time I was going through all this torment. She was trying to call me. You might think it was a coincidence, but I really feel God was saving my life. Well I asked her to please come home, let's work this out. We can work this out. I don't care what's gone on between us; God can do it. She said I want to ask you one thing, "Were you calling my name?"

Stephanie: I actually audibly heard Joe three times call my name out. There was maybe 25-miles distance between the two of us. And in the natural there was no way I could have heard

Joe. It was a supernatural thing God allowed. I really didn't understand God's word in *Genesis 2:24*, God made them one flesh, bone of each other's bone and flesh of each other's flesh. At that moment we were experiencing a one flesh encounter. God allowed the walls and the hardness and the distance to come down. God allowed me to hear my husband's heart crying out on my behalf.

Through the years and through the healing we've gone through I can really appreciate and understand what happened to me that night. I understand the grace of God. He even allowed me to hear Joe's heart to save me, and bring me back to repentance to the Lord. God also wanted me to hear his voice so Joe would not take his life. There was a double protection there. God was looking after our one flesh relationship.

Genesis 2:24 (NKJV)
Therefore a man shall leave his father and mother and be joined to his wife, and they shall become one flesh.

Our One Flesh relationship is a relationship blending us together body, soul and spirit making us one.

Ephesians 5:30-33 (NKJV)
For we are members of His body, of His flesh and of His bones. [31] "For this reason a man shall leave his father and mother and be joined to his wife, and the two shall become one flesh." [32] This is a great mystery, but I speak concerning Christ and the church.

<u>Joe</u>: I praise God now that Jesus did what He did for us. We know he can and wants to do those things for you. God's Word is true.

I remember using this scripture, 1 *Corinthians 7:4* "The wife has not power of her own body, but the husband and likewise also hath not power over his own body, but the wife." So I felt like well if I had power over my wife's body then the alien couldn't have her. I had to have her and I believed on those scriptures. I know some people now look at that and they say well that might be taking things a little bit too far. At this point I guess I don't really care what they think, because I know God's Word was and is true. It worked for us. It wasn't the delivery of the word it was the fact of believing the word.

Romans 10:17(NKJV)
So then faith comes by hearing, and hearing by the word of God.

I had to do the spiritual warfare. I had to believe the scriptures. I read through the Book of Hosea in the Bible. I saw Gods heart for marriage. Hosea's story showed the love he had for his wife Gomer. I saw what God's heart really was for our marriage. I had to believe God's power was strong enough to heal our marriage. I remember when Stephanie did come home after the situation of hearing my voice. She was submitting to God. We needed to be obedient to His word and that's how He started to heal us. That's how the healing process started. Healing was then released.

Stephanie: After two weeks time had passed after the incident where I heard Joe calling out my name, I had no peace at all in my heart. The Holy Spirit kept convicting and convicting. I really didn't want to come home because I felt like I loved this other person. We know now that since God is love, adultery can never be love. I felt nothing for Joe whatsoever. I felt sorry for him, but I didn't feel any love for him. I did feel the conviction of the Holy Spirit. Finally the conviction won out over my own flesh. The power of Satan, the demonic oppression was holding on to me had to let go!

I remember packing up the car with all my belongings and all the kid's belongings while the other person was at work.

I knew I had to go home if I wanted to get my life right with God. It seemed pretty impossible to me. My emotions were so messed up. The flesh was reigning. I felt my spirit man had completely died. I remember putting the kids in the car and I starting to drive home on the highway. As we were coming home on I-25 we almost had a near fatal accident. I believe it would have been a fatal accident. A car swerved out in front of my car. God was there and protected me. I felt like even that was a last ditch effort of Satan trying to destroy me and the kids before I had even reached home. I remember coming home and being in the house and thinking what am I doing here? I don't love him! I love this other person. I don't want to be here. I know I'm in sin. I want to get my life right. I was crying out to God saying God I don't love Joe, but somehow I trust you that you're going to make this right.

The first five, six, seven months were pretty rough. There was such a barrier between Joe and me. I started to build my relationship again with the Lord and started to get my heart right.

Joe: I knew Stephanie didn't like me; as a matter of fact she says she didn't love me. She pretty much hated my guts at the time. I knew that and that was kinda hard to live with I guess. I also knew God's word was true. I really believed God would – could put love, and I say back into our relationship, but really we wanted something new; we didn't want what we had before because what we had before I don't think was based on love. We were back together, but I remember I did not actually trust Stephanie. We had gone through all these things, the abuse, the torment I had put her through. I was unable to trust her because of the adultery. I could not trust it would not happen again, but I wasn't only not trusting her, I wasn't trusting God.

We came to a point where after a few months we actually started to pull apart again. We actually did get separated again. The Lord showed me how I had actually destroyed Stephanie. I'll never forget how he showed me a vision of a flower – I can see it to this day; it was purple and white and yellow. How I had crushed the flower. He showed me the flower was Stephanie. I had not really gone to Him and let Him start to heal our relationship. I remember we were living together and trying to get things back together. We were actually going to church all the time, going to every meeting we could go to, we were reading the Word. We were listening to tapes about marriage. We thought we were on the right track, but we really weren't totally. We still didn't have oneness together. We weren't sharing intimately with one another, letting God's Word work on the inside of us. I wasn't letting God do things to strengthen my own relationship with Him. At that point, I think I was really idolizing our marriage. I was worshipping Stephanie. I was worshipping the marriage relationship rather than God. I was not letting Him come in and do the things He wanted to do.

Stephanie: In Jeremiah 29:11 the word says "For I know the thoughts I think toward you sayeth the Lord, thoughts of peace and not of evil, to give you an expected end." As Joe shared he wasn't trusting God. He didn't have the peace of God to know God had His best for him. God could take care of me better than he could take care of me. Joe didn't trust because of the failures we had in our marriage. The disappointments we had. All the things we had done to one another. It was hard for him to even trust God. He came to the point of trusting God and giving up all claim and rights to me, releasing me over to the Lord. When he released me things began to change

Joe: I remember we really started to bond together. We finally had a one flesh relationship. We started to get healed more and more and sought ministries to help. We got on the right track. We started learning about what covenant was all about, what one flesh was all about. Then we really started to get healed. God's word started to really do something in our lives. We could have life in our relationship. That's what we desired. We actually were probably more opposite than anybody could be, but as God started to move in our lives we really started to see things in the same way. We saw God had a plan. God was there and He was using both of us in different ways to have His purpose fulfilled.

Stephanie: In Isaiah 43:18-19 says "Remember not the former things; neither consider the things of old. Behold I will do a new thing, now it shall spring forth; shall you not know it? I will even make a way in the wilderness and rivers in the desert." So really that's what God has done for us. He took away our past and the old nature and the hurts and the pain. He began to give us a new vision and a new hope for our marriage. We were able to forgive one another and forgive ourselves.

2 Timothy 2:21(NKJV)
[21] Therefore if anyone cleanses himself from the latter, he will be a vessel for honor, sanctified and useful for the Master, prepared for every good work.

Psalm 103:12 (NKJV)
As far as the east is from the west, So far has He removed our transgressions from us.

<u>Joe</u>: We shared earlier the psychologists and the psychiatrists all said that there was no hope for us. They said we could never get over the things that we'd done to each other. But Jesus' blood shed over us could. He would make us clean and as white as snow. He gave us back the innocence. We felt the adulteries and sin before marriage had never even happened. We could relate to one another as if they didn't happen. Only God could do this miracle. We praise Him for that right now, we're here to tell you what God has done for us, He will do for you.

Revelation 12:11 (NKJV)
And they overcame him by the blood of the Lamb and by the word of their testimony, and they did not love their lives to the death.

Most people have heard the story of David and Goliath. We wanted to let tell you no matter what situation you're in today, God is there for you as He was for David. Goliath tormented the Israelites like the devil try's to do to our marriages. We need to treat the devil the way David treated

Goliath in *1 Samuel 17:4.1* The Word says "So the Philistine came, and began drawing near to David, and the man who bore the shield went before him. And when the Philistine looked about and saw David, he disdained him, for he was only a youth, ruddy and good-looking."

The enemy would like all of us to think we're nothing, that we're nothing in the eyes of man; we're nothing in the eyes of God; that we're basically no good. We are much more than what the devil wants us to think. We're something God has made and God holds us in high esteem. He has a purpose for us. "So the Philistine said to David, 'Am I a dog that you come to me with sticks?' And the Philistine cursed David by his gods. And the Philistine said to David, 'Come to me, and I will give your flesh to the birds of the air and the beasts of the field!' Then David said to the Philistine, 'You come to me with a sword, with a spear, and with a javelin. But I come to you in the name of the LORD of hosts, the God of the armies of Israel, whom you have defied. This day the LORD will deliver you into my hand, and I will strike you and take your head from you. And this day I will give the carcasses of the camp of the Philistines to the birds of the air and the wild beasts of the earth, that all the earth may know that there is a God in Israel. Then all this assembly shall know that the LORD does not save with sword and spear; but for the battle is the LORD's, and He will give you into our hands." And that's why we're here today and that's why we give our testimony as many times and in as many places as we can to turn what the enemy has used against us. Turn it against him and let God heal your life and your land. "So it was, when the Philistine arose and came and drew near to meet David that David hurried and ran toward the army to meet the Philistine." And that's what we need to do, we need to run toward whatever that Goliath is in our life; whether it be sickness, whether it be emotional strain, whether it be financial disaster, we run towards the problem with God's word and we defeat the enemy. "Then David put his hand in his bag and took out a stone; and he slung it and struck the Philistine in his forehead, so that the stone sank into his forehead, and he fell on his face to the earth.

So David prevailed over the Philistine with a sling and a stone, and struck the Philistine and killed him. But there was no sword in the hand of David." Well that's where David really got his victory. He took the same sword that was coming against him and used it against the enemy. "Therefore David ran and stood over the Philistine, took his sword and drew it out of its sheath and killed him, and cut off his head with it. And when the Philistines saw that their champion was dead, they fled." And we're saying right here and now that anything the enemy has done in your marriage, you can take it and you can turn it against him. You can use the enemy's sword which is the sin that tried to destroy you and through your testimony use it against the enemy. Now instead use God's Sword which is His word and redemption to see healing in your and the lives of others. We ask the Lord that He would bless your marriage.

The God of Israel, the same one that healed our Land will heal you. Let Him do the work.

Stephanie: Do not look at the circumstances, look beyond them. Know now God's power is able. He's there to heal you. God wants to give back whatever Satan has stolen away from you. In 2 Corinthians 1:4 the word says "who comforts us in all our tribulation, that we may be able to comfort them which are in any trouble by the same comfort where with we ourselves are comforted of God." We have shared with you that God did a miraculous thing in our life. We have shared God will comfort you with the same comfort God has given to us. We release the faith to you to believe that God will do it for you.

Joe: Amen. In Jeremiah 32:39 the word says "then I will give them one heart and one way, that they may fear me forever, for the good of them and the children after them. And I will make an everlasting covenant with them that I will not turn away from doing them good; but I will put my fear in their hearts so that they will not depart from me. Yes, I will rejoice over them to do them good, and I will assuredly plant them in this land with all my heart and with all my soul." We bless you today in Jesus' name.

You have the answers in Him. We are overcomers. He gives us hope.

Ephesians 1:7
*In Him we have **redemption** through His blood, the forgiveness of sins, according to the riches of His grace*

*The DeMott's testimony brings hope and encouragement to any marriage, and they minister to couples through teaching, the prophetic, and their own transparency. Joe and Stephanie have shared their story on the **700 Club** as well as TBN's **Praise the Lord** show, and many other Christian television and radio programs. They have a unique ministry niche to nine nations in Italian through their own broadcast on www.radiofedeitalia.it*

Joe and Stephanie have been married since 1975 and have four grown children and six grandchildren. Joe is a retired 30 year veteran Detective of the Denver Police Department where he worked in the Homicide Unit for eleven years. The DeMott's were called to marriage ministry in 1986 and have ministered all over the US as well as in Ethiopia, Denmark, Sweden, Italy, Scotland, Switzerland, Singapore, Germany and England as well as the U.S. the most recent trip being to Cuba. The DeMott's are also ministering in Pakistan and the Ukraine via online Breakthrough Meetings. Many countries have contacted us and we are developing ways to minister to them.

Please contact us for further resources or help in your marriage

PO BOX 7832
Broomfield, Colorado 80021
Office: 303-465-0342
Cell: 720-351-6211
info@missionaries2marriages.com
www.missionaries2marriages.com
Also look for us on Facebook and Youtube through our website

You can also give to our ministry on our website. We would appriciate your gift and as you Partner with us you will be touching couples and families throughout the world. We are a 501C3 ministry.

 2 Corinthians 8:23 (CJB) *As for Titus, he is my partner who works with me on your behalf; and the other brothers with him are emissaries of the congregations and bring honor to the Messiah.*

www.ingramcontent.com/pod-product-compliance
Lightning Source LLC
Chambersburg PA
CBHW071550080526
44588CB00011B/1854